D0205342

LEADERSHIP

Quotations to inspire and celebrate the leader in all of us

Compiled by Dan Zadra
Designed by Kobi Yamada
and Steve Potter

COM·PEN·DI·UM™
Publishing

LYNNWOOD, WASHINGTON

ACKNOWLEDGEMENTS

These quotations were gathered lovingly but unscientifically over several years and/or contributed by many friends or acquaintances. Some arrived, and survived in our files, on scraps of paper and may therefore be imperfectly worded or attributed. To the authors, contributors and original sources, our thanks, and where appropriate, our apologies.
—The editors

CREDITS

Compiled by Dan Zadra
Designed by Kobi Yamada and Steve Potter

ISBN 1-888387-95-5

Printed in China

LEADERSHIP

A Gift to Inspire and Celebrate Your Achievements

We rise by lifting others.
—Robert Green Ingersoll

Somewhere in this book is an ironic reminder that "leadership cannot be learned by just reading a book." That is very true. Becoming a trusted and effective leader is a lifelong process of discovery. But nothing compresses the process faster than hearing the hard-earned lessons of other leaders.

Some of the simplest and most powerful of those lessons are included in these pages—and most of them require no further explanation.

Here's a three-word lesson:
"Don't point—lead."

And a five-word lesson:
"You can't lead with memos."

And a six-word lesson:
"If your horse dies, get off."

The most important lessons of all, however, are the ones that remind us that the world is changing, and that leadership must change with it. Our world has become far too fast and too complicated for any one person to run the show. The days of the Lone Ranger are over. Every organization worth its salt now realizes that every person in every position can lead, and must be encouraged to do so. As Donald McGannon puts it, "Everyone leads. Leadership is action, not position."

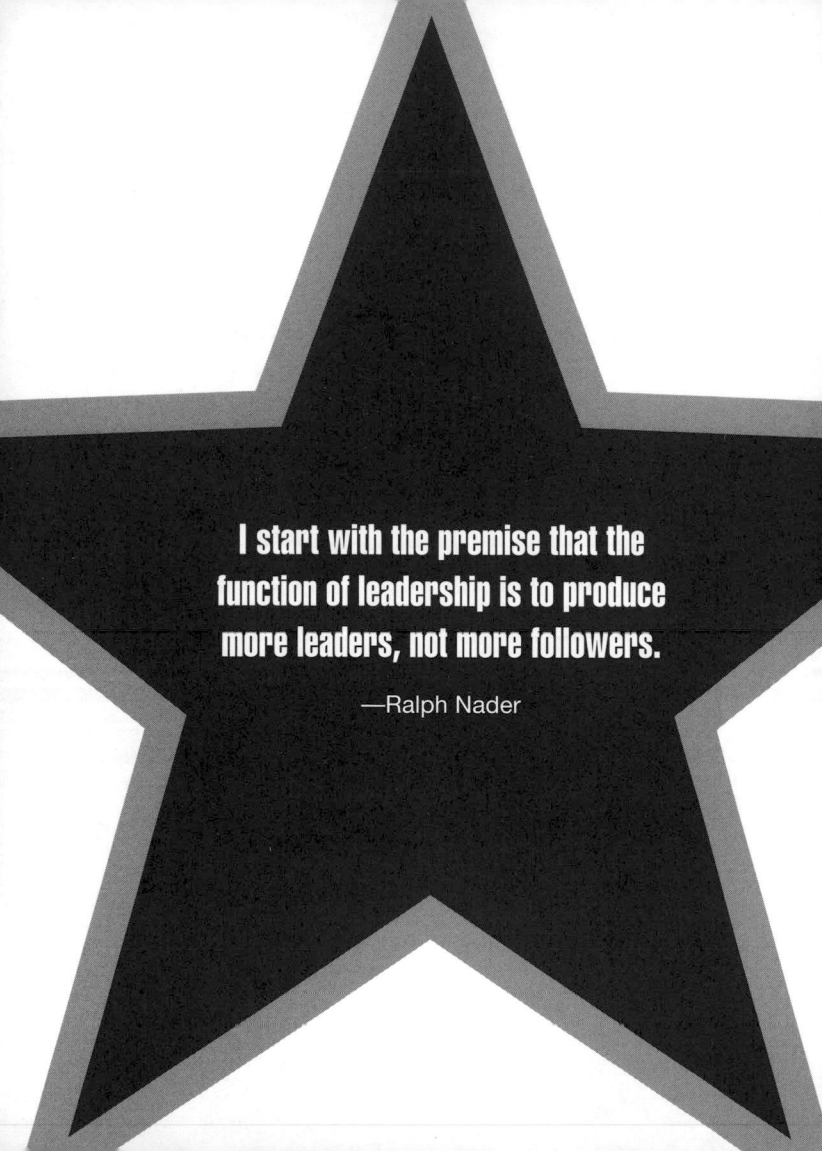

I start with the premise that the function of leadership is to produce more leaders, not more followers.

—Ralph Nader

In times like these,
all can lead and ought
to be invited to do so.

MATTHEW FOX

Everyone leads.
Leadership is action,
not position.

DONALD H. MCGANNON

LEADERSHIP

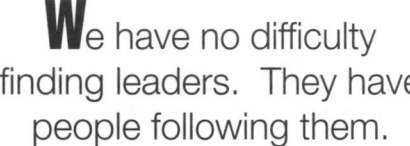We have no difficulty finding leaders. They have people following them.

WILLIAM GORE

Leaders don't flock. You find them one at a time.

ROSS PEROT

Leadership cannot
be learned by simply
reading about it.

HENRY MINTZBERG

Very few natural-born
leaders turn up in
the workplace. People
become leaders.

MILTON COTTER

LEADERSHIP

You can always develop expertise. First, discover your mission.

CHARLES GARFIELD

Determine that the thing shall be done, and then you shall find the way.

ABRAHAM LINCOLN

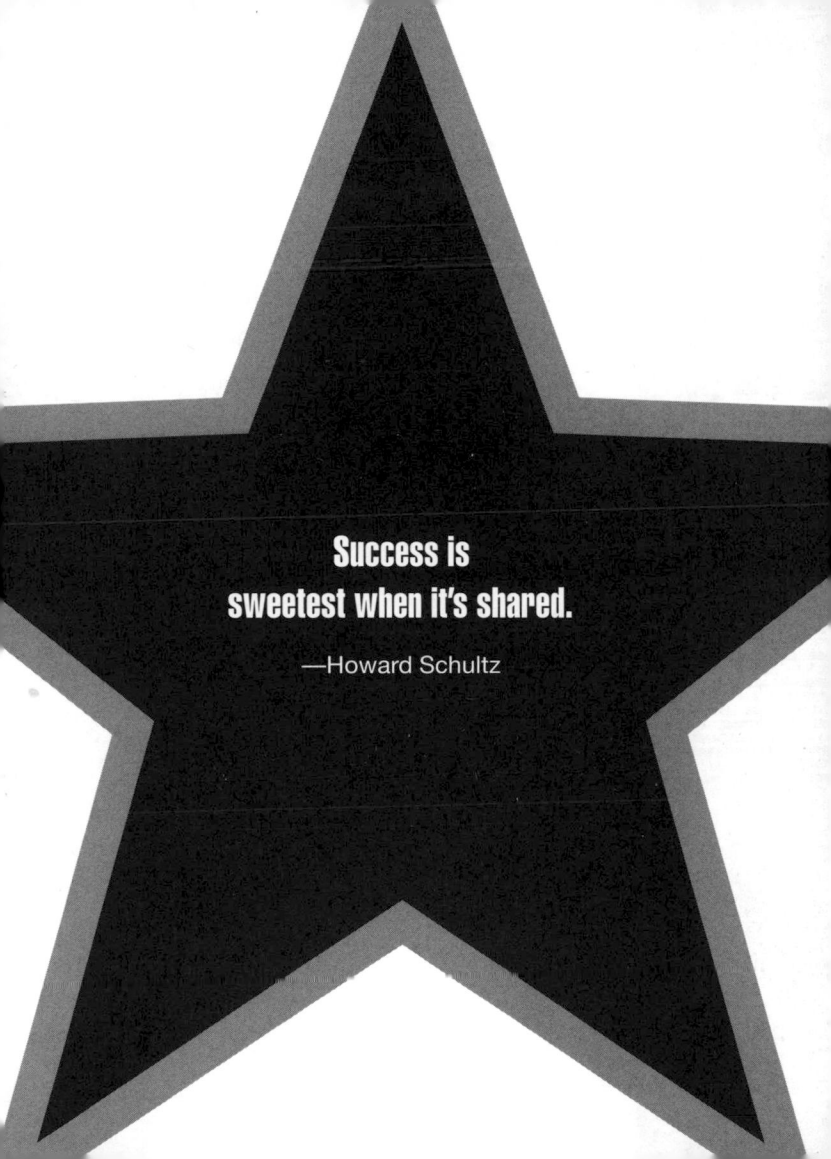

**Success is
sweetest when it's shared.**

—Howard Schultz

Shared vision is essential. When the blind lead the blind… get out of the way.

CARLOS MENTA

That Vision statement up on the wall is your credo. If you're not going to live by it, then tear it down.

DICK KAMM

Vision and mission motivate.

ANDREW BENNETT

★

A vision is not a vision
unless is says yes to some
ideas and no to others,
inspires people and is a
reason to get out of bed
in the morning and
come to work.

GIFFORD PINCHOT

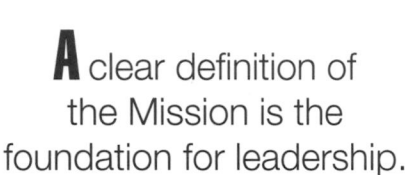

A clear definition of the Mission is the foundation for leadership.

PETER DRUCKER

Most people manage the "what" and the "how." Leaders manage the "why."

PAT HORNER

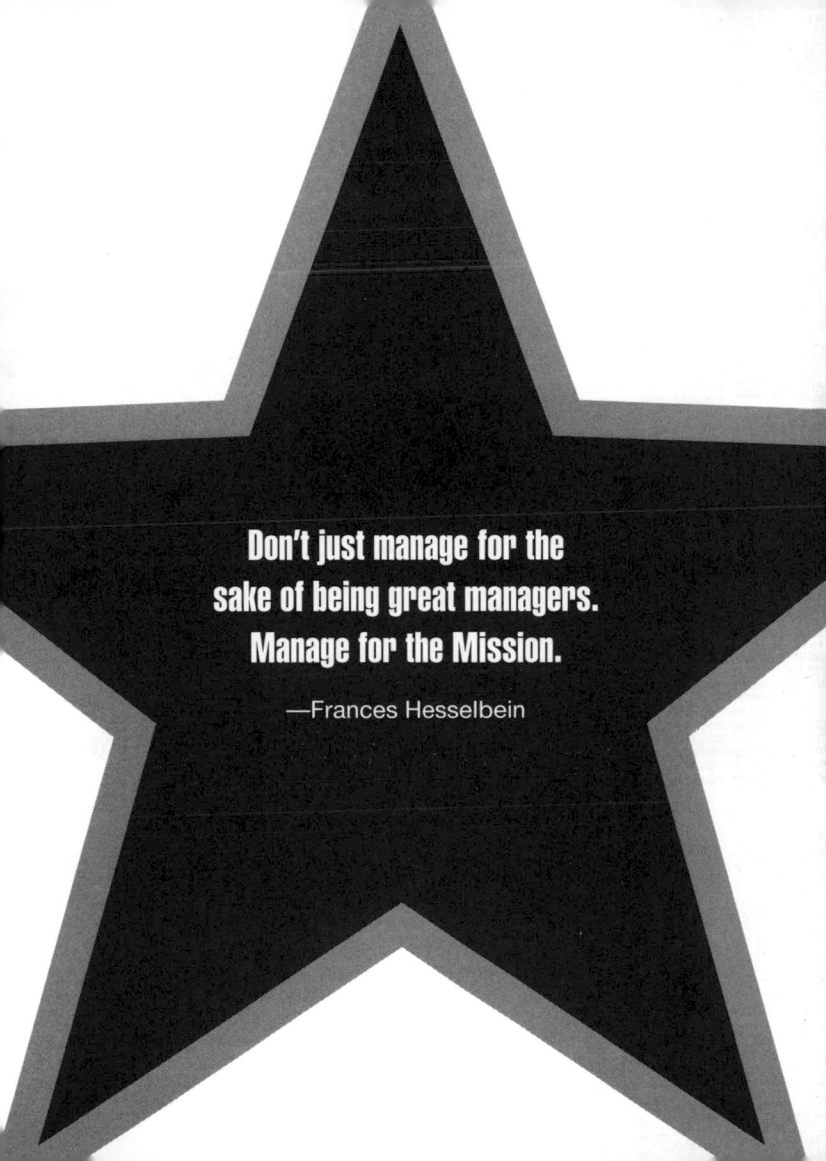

Don't just manage for the
sake of being great managers.
Manage for the Mission.

—Frances Hesselbein

LEADERSHIP

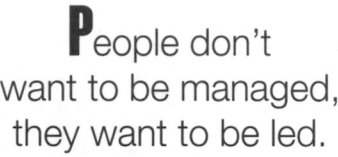

People don't
want to be managed,
they want to be led.

HARRY GRAY

You cannot manage
men into battle. You manage
things; you lead people.

ADMIRAL GRACE HOPPER

We can do more
than lead, we can inspire.

DAN ZADRA

Managers light
a fire under people;
leaders light a fire
in people.

KATHY AUSTIN

LEADERSHIP

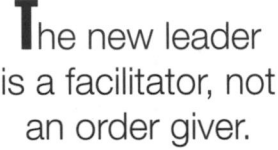

The new leader
is a facilitator, not
an order giver.

JOHN NAISBITT

It is commitment,
not authority, that
produces results.

WILLIAM GORE

You need to learn
to level with people,
without leveling them.

—Foster Davis

LEADERSHIP

An enormous
number of managers
have stopped leading—
have basically retired
on the job.

PETER DRUCKER

People who are resting
on their laurels are wearing
them on the wrong end.

MALCOLM KUSHNER

We have to earn
our wings every day.

FRANK BORMAN, U.S. ASTRONAUT

Leadership is not bestowed—
it is yours only as long as
it is continuously earned.

B.J. MARSHAL

Don't point. Lead!

PAUL TRIPP

You cannot lead
where you do not go.

DON WARD

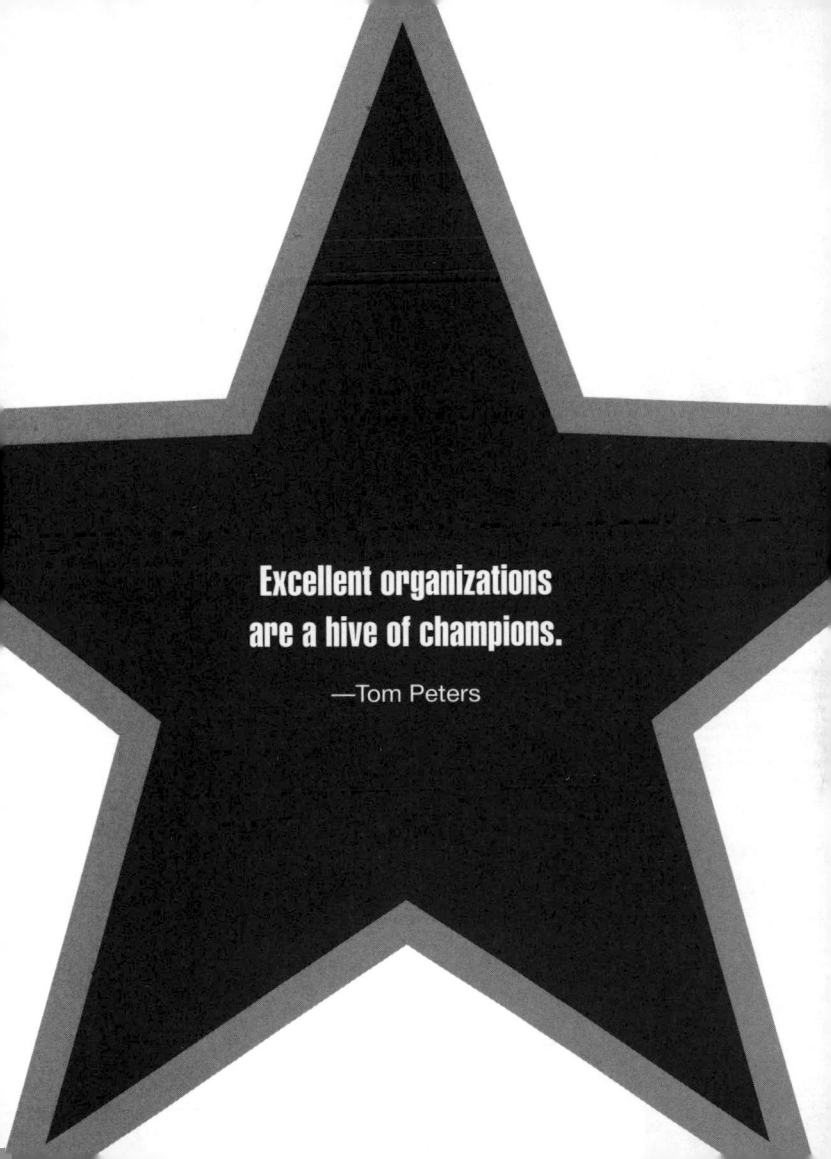

**Excellent organizations
are a hive of champions.**

—Tom Peters

LEADERSHIP

Life is made up
of constant calls
to action.

LEARNED HAND

Your people can't
answer a call that
isn't made.

DON WARD

So much of what
we call management
consists in making it difficult
for people to work.

PETER DRUCKER

The leader is the "servant"
who removes the obstacles
that prevent people from
doing their jobs.

MAX DEPREE

People tend to resist that which is forced upon them. People tend to support that which they help to create.

VINCE PFAFF

Those convinced against their will are of the same opinion still.

HENRY HODEL

Keep in the
forefront of your mind
that people want to be
themselves.

MARK DAVID

People don't resist
change, so much as they
resist being changed.

PETER SCHOLTES

When people
show you who they are,
believe them.

—Maya Angelou

There are many
wonderful things that
will never be done if
you do not do them.

HONORABLE CHARLES D. GILL

You can do anything,
but you cannot do everything.
Create your team.

DON WARD

There is no such thing
as an insignificant task,
job or person.

DON WARD

Hold your
frontline people high.
No, higher than that.

FRANK VIZZARE

Unexpressed
competence appears
much the same as
incompetence.

JAY HALL

Everyone you meet is
a potential winner; some
are disguised as losers.
Don't be fooled by
their appearances.

KEN BLANCHARD

"Great people"
don't equal
"great teams."

TOM PETERS

You need both
competency *and* chemistry.
Those who are not team
players will have to go.

JEANNE GREENBERG

**There is always
a second right answer.**

—Roger von Oech

LEADERSHIP

Control freaks don't
grow good companies.

JEFFREY TIMMONS

Resign as general
manager of the universe
and trust your team.

LARRY EISENBERG

Celebrate what you
want to see more of.

TOM PETERS

Throw the spotlight
into every nook and cranny
of your company and
catch people in the act
of doing things right.

BILL MEYER

LEADERSHIP

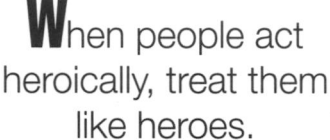

When people act
heroically, treat them
like heroes.

JEFF GOFORTH

Treat people greatly,
and they will show
themselves great.

RALPH WALDO EMERSON

The leader is making a way out of no way.

—Henry Louis Gates

We rise by lifting others.

ROBERT GREEN INGERSOLL

In order for me to look good, everybody around me has to look good.

DORIS DRURY

A good leader
takes more of his share
of the blame, and less
of his share of the credit.

ROB GILBERT

The leader is not the one
in the spotlight, but the one
leading the applause.

VINCE PFAFF

LEADERSHIP

Morale is
self-esteem in action.

AVERY WEISMAN

People who feel good
about themselves get
good results.

KEN BLANCHARD

As you enter
positions of trust
and power, dream a little
before you think.

TONI MORRISON

Dreaming and
seeing precede doing.

MARGARET E. SANGSTER

Never mistake ideals for ideas.

—Don Ward

Don't be frightened of new ideas. Be frightened of the old ones.

JOHN CAGE

It's easy to come up with new ideas. The hard part is letting go of something that worked for you two years ago, but which is no longer useful.

ROGER VON OECH

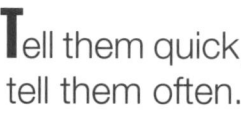

Tell them quick,
tell them often.

WILLIAM WRIGLEY, JR.

Communicate everything
you possibly can to your team.
The more they understand,
the more they'll care.
Once they care, there's
no stopping them.

SAM WALTON

Trust your crazy ideas.

★

Every new idea
looks crazy at first.

Sacred cows make great steaks.

MARK TWAIN

The worst thing you can hear in an organization is, "We've always done it this way."

DON WARD

Trade minds with your people.
Ideas build on ideas.

DAN ZADRA

The great leader is
the one who makes
two ideas grow where
only one grew before.

ELBERT HUBBARD

If he works for you,
you work for him.

JAPANESE PROVERB

If you honor and serve
the people who work
for you, they will honor
and serve you.

MARY KAY ASH

The best leaders are not interested in having their own way, but in finding the best way.

WILFRED PETERSON

The aim of the great leader is not to get people to think more highly of the leader. It's to get people to think more highly of themselves.

BOB MOAWAD

When you're through learning,
you're through.

—Vernon Law

Leaders are not
obsessed with rules.
Any fool can make a rule.

HENRY DAVID THOREAU

★

They trashed the rules and
found new ways to win.

MARK ROMAN

51

LEADERSHIP

It's what you learn after you know it all that counts.

JOHN WOODEN

Those who think they know it all have no way of finding out they don't.

LEO BUSCAGLIA

To stay ahead,
you must have your
next idea waiting
in the wings.

ROSABETH MOSS KANTER

Write down one idea
every day. At the end of
the year you'll have more
ideas than most people
have in a lifetime.

GIL ATKINSON

LEADERSHIP

You can't lead your
people with memos
for very long.

PAUL HARCOURT

Leaders come out from behind
the desk and openly engage in
emotional issues that connect
them with their followers.

JOHN ZENGER

In the heroic
organizations, people
mentor each other
unselfishly.

DON GALER

Organizations learn
only through individuals
who learn.

PETER SENGE

Make someone's day:
Ask for an opinion.

—Gil Atkinson

Search for ways
to give every employee
more control over their
piece of the business.

BOB GILBERTSON

Delegating means letting
others become the experts
and hence the best.

TIM FIRNSTAHL

57

LEADERSHIP

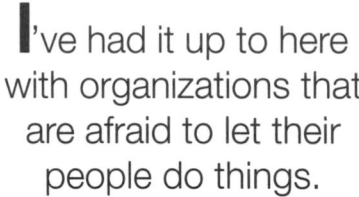

I've had it up to here with organizations that are afraid to let their people do things.

AL GREY

Hire the best. Pay them fairly. Communicate frequently. Provide challenges and rewards. Believe in them. Get out of their way—they'll knock your socks off.

MARY ANN ALLISON

Leaders excite action
and welcome accountability.
Without action a good decision
has little meaning in the world.

DAN ZADRA

The perfect bureaucrat
somehow manages to
make no decisions and
escapes all responsibility.

BROOKS ATKINSON

I beg each of you to
develop a passionate
and public hatred of
bureaucracy.

TOM PETERS

Nothing is less productive
than to make more efficient
that which should not
be done at all.

PETER DRUCKER

Eradicate petty rules
and annoyances.

TOM PETERS

Nothing short-circuits
good people and great
service faster than
"company policy."

MARY KAY ASH

LEADERSHIP

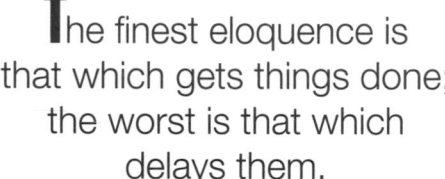

The finest eloquence is that which gets things done; the worst is that which delays them.

DAVID LLOYD GEORGE

Every management layer you can strip away makes you more responsive.

JOHN R. WHITNEY

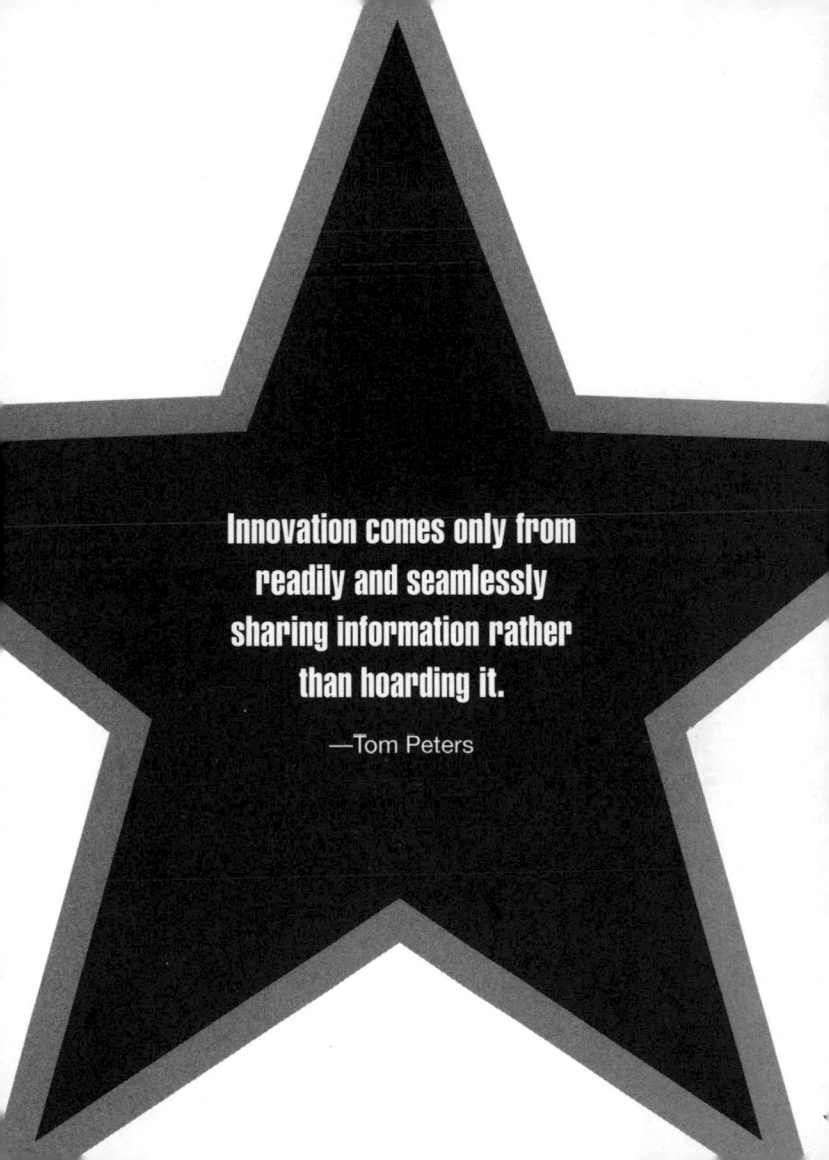

Innovation comes only from readily and seamlessly sharing information rather than hoarding it.

—Tom Peters

I've never been bashful about asking for help.

TED TURNER

Asking for help is not a weakness, it's a strength.

MARTHA MANNING

The one thing a leader
cannot withhold from people
in the Information Age
is information.

CARLA O'DELL

Bricks and mortar
don't ask why.
But people do, and
people deserve answers.

JOHN GUASPARI

Why is it that when anything goes without saying, it never does?

MARCELENE COX

The less you talk, the more you're listened to.

ABIGAIL VAN BUREN

Ask your team,
they know the answer.

CHUCK CARLSON

Somebody has the
solution, and no one will
listen to that person.

KARL ALBRECHT

Don't overreact
to the grumblers
and trouble makers.

WARREN G. BENNIS

Most of the trouble
in the world is caused
by people who want
to feel important.

T.S. ELIOT

Don't make excuses—
make good.

ELBERT HUBBARD

Acknowledging a mistake
just shows you're
smarter today than
you were yesterday.

KEYNOTE

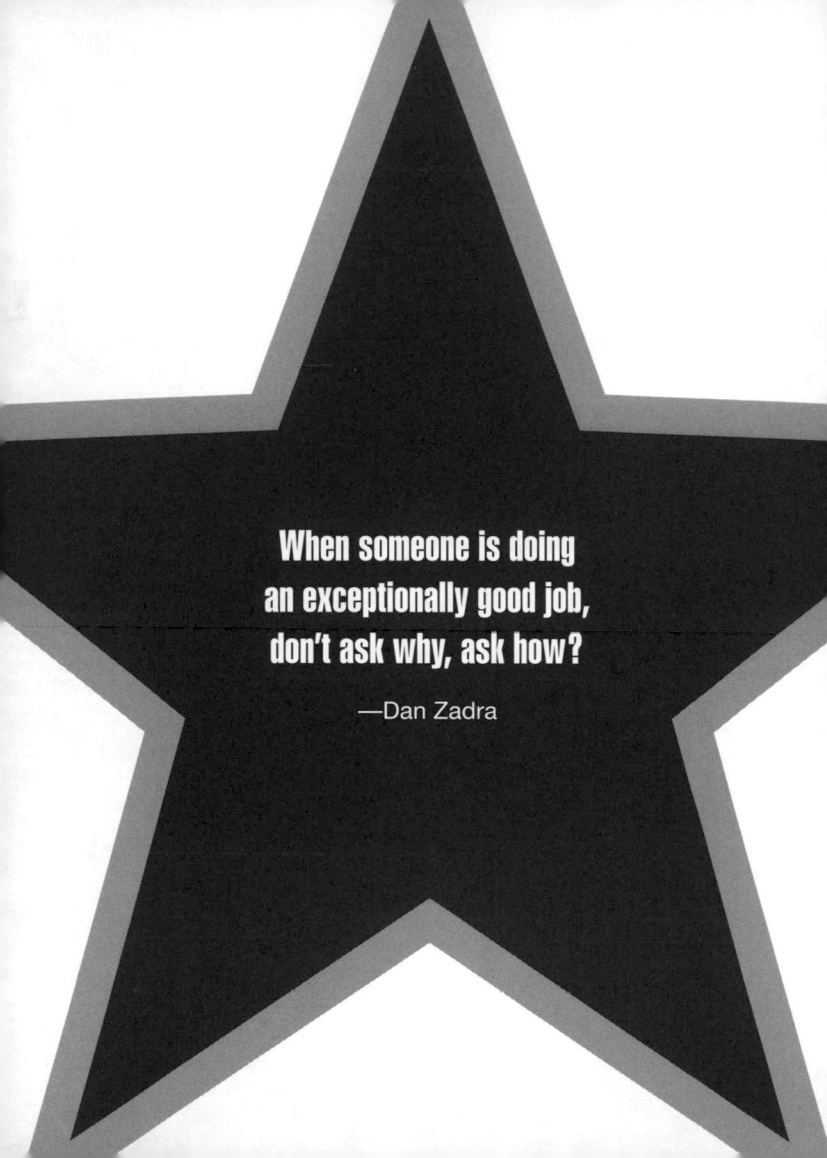

When someone is doing
an exceptionally good job,
don't ask why, ask how?

—Dan Zadra

Walk in right now
and clear the air.

HARRY GRAY

Nothing is settled until
it is settled right.

LOUIS BRANDEIS

Leaders ask questions.
Asking the right questions
takes as much skill as
giving the right answers.

ROBERT HALF

Answer the question,
"How and where will I
commit my resources?"
The answer is your strategy.

R. HENRY MIGLIONE

Good leaders are scarce,
so I'm following myself.

Leadership is a potent
combination of strategy
and character. But if you
must be without one,
be without strategy.

LEADERSHIP

People who never get carried away should be.

MALCOLM FORBES

If you're working in an organization that is NOT enthusiastic, energetic, creative, clever, curious, and just plain fun, you've got serious troubles.

TOM PETERS

Passion persuades.

ANITA RODDICK

★

Energy rightly
applied and directed can
accomplish anything.

NELLIE BLY

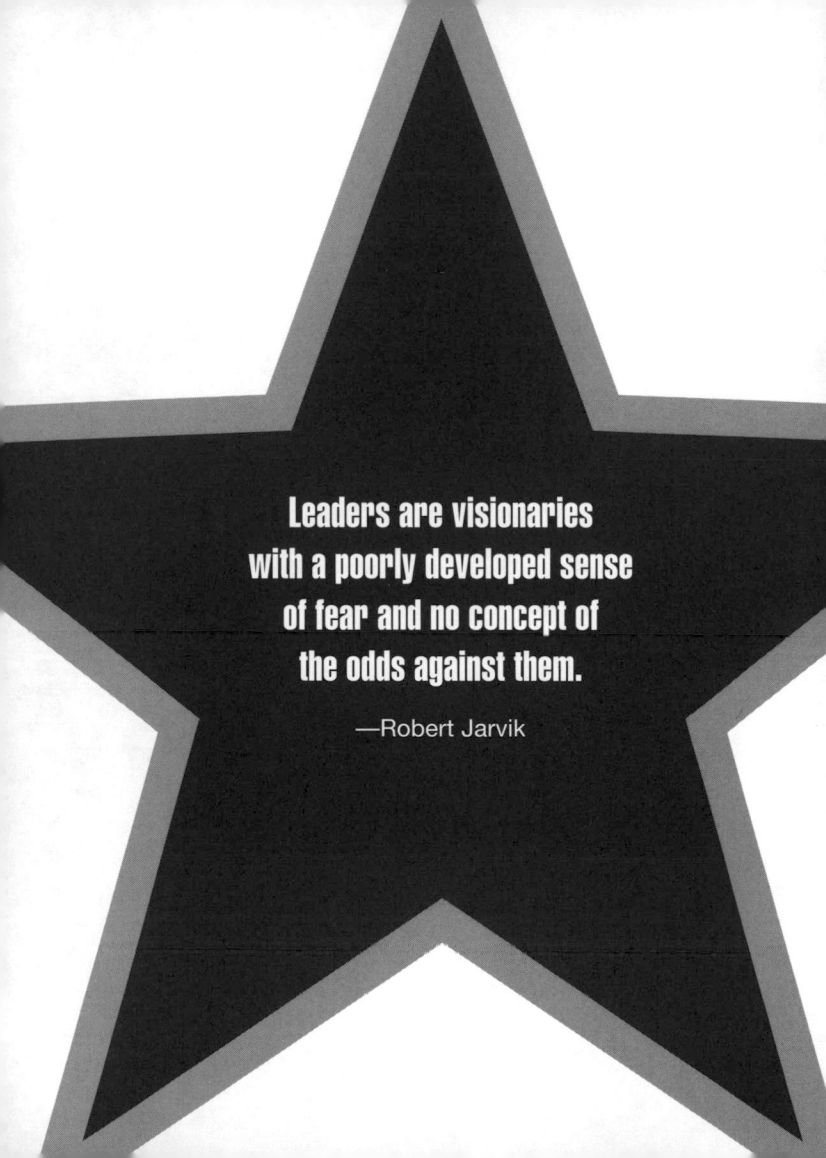

Leaders are visionaries
with a poorly developed sense
of fear and no concept of
the odds against them.

—Robert Jarvik

Do you want to be
a power in the world?
Then be yourself.

RALPH WALDO EMERSON

There is only one you.
God wanted you to
be you. Don't you dare
change just because
you're outnumbered.

CHARLES SWINDOLL

LEADERSHIP

To lead a symphony,
you must occasionally turn
your back on the crowd.

JOHN OLDS

If you are going to have
ideas ahead of the times,
you will have to get used to
living with the fact that most
people are going to believe
you are in the wrong.

BRUCE LLOYD

Leaders live in the
present—but concentrate
on the future.

JAMES HAYES

The great leaders
don't resist innovation,
they symbolize it.

DAVID OGILVY

LEADERSHIP

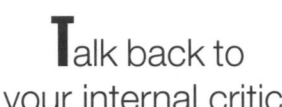

Talk back to
your internal critic.

ROBERT MCKAIN

Tell the negative committee
that meets in your head to
sit down and shut up.

KATHY KENDALL

In the book of leadership,
you can't find the answers
in the back of the book.

DENNIS OLESON

Sometimes you just have to
trust your intuition.

BILL GATES

Being responsible sometimes means pissing people off.

MICHAEL VIGIL

Some people will get angry with your decisions. It's inevitable, if you're honorable.

COLIN POWELL

The best leaders gain authority
by giving it away.

—James Stockdale

LEADERSHIP

Aquila non captat muscas:
*The eagle does not
catch flies.*

ERASMUS

Stay big-hearted,
generous and magnanimous
with your people. Life is too
short to be little.

HUGH LYON

Heart, instinct, principles.

BLAISE PASCAL

Never compromise yourself.
You are all you've got.

BETTY FORD

Trust is a treasured item.

MARY AUGUSTINE

Trust is the conviction
that the leader means
what he or she says.
It comes from consistency
and integrity. Trust opens
the door to change.

PETER DRUCKER

Tremendous humility
comes from others
having faith in you.

DAG HAMMERSKJOLD

Arrogance is
a sure and certain
symptom of low
self-esteem.

GIL ATKINSON

LEADERSHIP

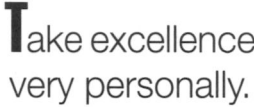

Take excellence
very personally.

SCOTT JOHNSON

★

Be so good they
can't ignore you.

JERRY DUNN

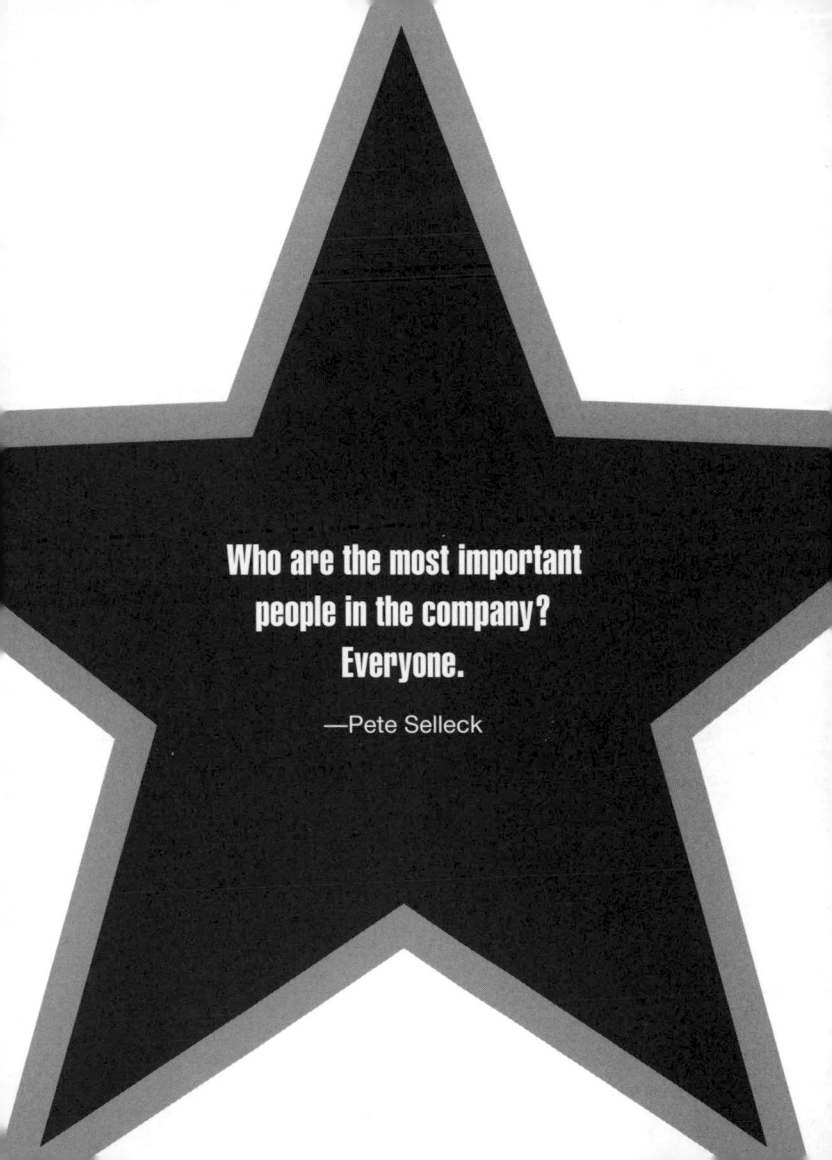

Who are the most important people in the company? Everyone.

—Pete Selleck

LEADERSHIP

People look to you
for heat as well as light.

GIL ATKINSON

The people who shape
our lives have the ability
to communicate a vision
or a quest or a joy
or a mission.

ANTHONY ROBBINS

We have to get
people excited again
about using their talents.

PATRICIA CARRIGAN

High motivation and
talent will always beat
mere talent alone.

NORMAN GUSTINE

LEADERSHIP

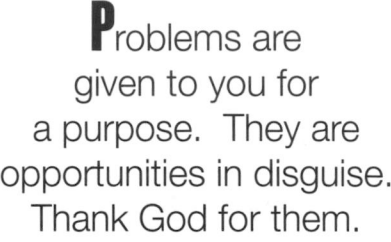

Problems are
given to you for
a purpose. They are
opportunities in disguise.
Thank God for them.

DON WARD

I have fresh problems
flown in daily.

RICHARD LEWIS

When you can't
solve the problem,
manage it.

ROBERT SCHULLER

Every problem is
smaller when discussed.

GAIL MANN

Never try to solve
all the problems at once—
make them line up
for you one-by-one.

RICHARD SLOMA

Nothing is particularly hard
if you divide it into small jobs.

HENRY FORD

Good leaders are able to
recognize a problem before
it becomes an emergency.

ARNOLD GLASGOW

The leader of the
not too distant future will
be rated wholly by his or her
ability to anticipate issues
rather than to meet them
as they come.

HOWARD COONLEY

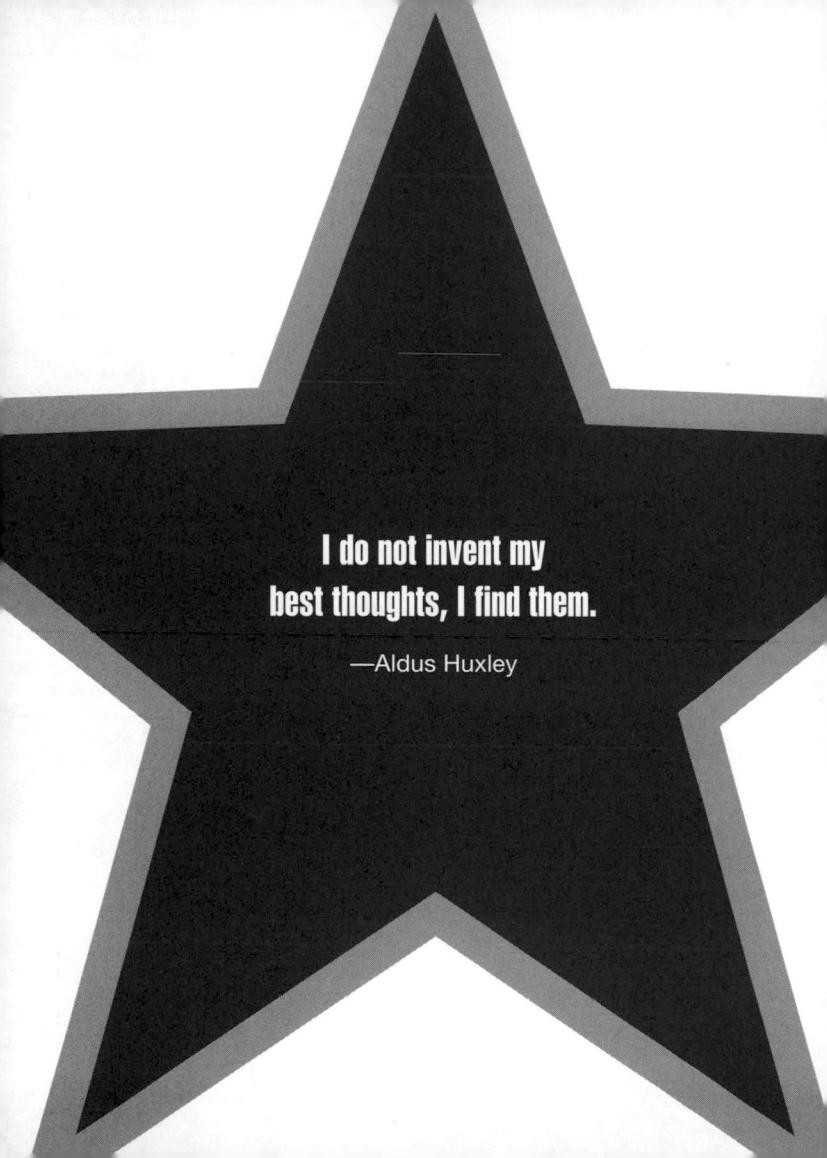

I do not invent my
best thoughts, I find them.

—Aldus Huxley

Failure is one sure way
of mapping the future.

DWAYNE KOONTZ

The fastest way to
succeed is to double
your failure rate.

THOMAS J. WATSON

LEADERSHIP

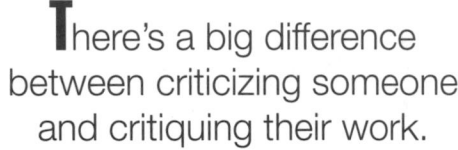

There's a big difference between criticizing someone and critiquing their work.

ANDREW S. GROVE

A failure is an event, never a person.

WILLIAM D. BROWN

Post-mortems on defeats
are never very useful
unless they give insights
for the future.

JAMES RESTON

Quickly forgive every
honest mistake. Call it
a training expense—
and learn from it.

KONOSUKE MATSUSHITA

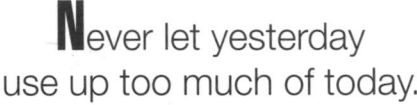

Never let yesterday
use up too much of today.

ERMA PHILLIPS

The crisis of yesterday
is the joke of tomorrow.

H.G. WELLS

Always know in your heart that you are far bigger than anything that can happen to you.

DAN ZADRA

There will be ebbs and flows. Remember that the tide goes out, but it *always* comes back.

BOB MOAWAD

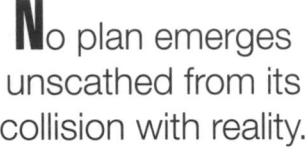

No plan emerges
unscathed from its
collision with reality.

HERBERT MEYER

Exploit a failure;
don't waste it.

CHARLES KETTERING

New ideas are not
born in a conforming
environment.

ROGER VON OECH

Treasure diversity.
Seek unity, not uniformity.
Strive for oneness,
not sameness.

DAN ZADRA

Age is not important
unless you're a cheese.

HELEN HAYES

★

Leadership is not necessarily
a function of age. Get some
young tigers and old lions
in your organization.

JOEL ROSS

Either do not
attempt at all, or
go through with it.

★

If you're going to take
Vienna, take Vienna.

LEADERSHIP

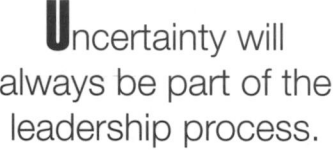

Uncertainty will always be part of the leadership process.

JOHN GABARRO

Leaders act decisively in the absence of certainty.

BERTRAND RUSSELL

The biggest obstacle to overcoming the odds is never challenging them.

ROB GILBERT

The what-if question begs an answer: What if we tried?

DALE DAUTEN

Fortune favors
the bold.

TERENCE

★

When you cannot
make up your mind which
of two evenly balanced
courses of action to take,
choose the bolder.

GENERAL W.J. SLIM

You always know
the right thing to do.
The hard part is doing it.

NORMAN SCHWARZKOPF

It's how you walk through
the fire that counts.

GEORGE LAZARES

Be prepared for everything.

DWIGHT EISENHOWER

Never think you've seen the last of anything.

EUDORA WELTY

Each dawn holds a
new hope for a new plan,
making the start of each
day the start of a new life.

GINA BLAIR

When the best leader's
work is done, the people say,
"We did it ourselves."

LAO-TSU

STAR ★ SERIES

Also available from
Compendium Publishing
are these spirited companion
books in the Star Series
of great quotations:

GOALS

MOTIVATION

TEAMWORK

These books may be ordered directly
from the publisher (800) 914-3327.
But please try your local bookstore first!

www.compendiuminc.com